The

Wit and Wisdom

of

Jimmy Carter

The
Wit and Wisdom
of
Jimmy Carter

Edited by

92
CAR.

BILL ADLER

CITADEL PRESS   SECAUCUS, N.J.

78-408

Published by Citadel Press
A division of Lyle Stuart Inc.
120 Enterprise Ave, Secaucus, N. J. 07094
In Canada: George J. McLeod Limited, Toronto
Manufactured in the United States of America

Photographs: *Wide World Photos*

Library of Congress Cataloging in Publication Data

Carter, Jimmy, 1924-
    The wit and wisdom of Jimmy Carter.

    1. Carter, Jimmy, 1924-   --Quotations. I. Adler,
Bill. II. Title.
E873.A58   973.926'092'4 [B]   77-1428
ISBN 0-8065-0563-X

The Wit and Wisdom of Jimmy Carter

Nothing describes a person better than his own words.

Such is the case with the man from Plains, the thirty-ninth President of the United States: Jimmy Carter.

Selected from speeches, writings, press conferences, interviews, and conversations—here is the wit and wisdom of the former peanut farmer, former Governor of Georgia, and thirty-ninth President of the United States.

This is Jimmy Carter talking about his faith, his family, his hopes, his fears, and his dreams.

Here is Jimmy Carter—on the record and off the record—speaking freely, often with wit, always with candor and honesty.

Here is a revealing portrait of a determined man in whose hands much of the world's destiny rests.

What is he really like? How does he think? What kind of man is the 39th President of the United States?

I believe the wit and wisdom of Jimmy Carter goes a long way toward answering that question.

BILL ADLER
NEW YORK CITY

EDITOR'S NOTE   *I am most grateful to Wendy Wilbert for her creative assistance. Without her this book would not have been possible.*

—B. A.

Contents

The

Wit and Wisdom

of

Jimmy Carter

The Carter Wit

During a speech at the University of Georgia, Carter said:
I found out when the program was prepared that Senator Kennedy was to speak last night. They charged $10 to attend the occasion. Senator William Brock from Tennessee is speaking to the Lamar Society at noon today. I found out that they charged $7.50 for this occasion. I spoke yesterday at noon, and I asked the Lamar Society officials, at the last moment, how much they were charging to come to the luncheon yesterday. They said they weren't charging anything. I said, "You mean they don't even have to pay for the lunch?" They said, "No, we're providing the lunch free."

So when my son Jack came and said, "Daddy, I think more of you than you thought I did; I'm paying $7.00 for two tickets to the luncheon," I figured that a $3.50 lunch ticket would salvage part of my ego, and that's really why I'm here today.

Athens, Georgia
May, 1974

In an interview with Norman Mailer, when told about Mailer's many marriages, alimony payments, etc., Carter said:

You've been married five times, and you have seven children.

Mailer nodded.

Well, good luck.

> Plains, Georgia
> September, 1976

Speaking before a crowd in Texas, Carter commented:

The thing that hurts is, if you are a suspect and if you don't have influence, if you are poor, you have a good chance of going to prison, but if you are rich you never see the inside of a prison.

I'm not trying to send the rich people to prison.

Appearing before a crowd in Dallas the day after his first television debate with Ford, Carter said:

Last night when I was commenting on the FBI and the CIA the sound went off for twenty-seven minutes. I should have known better.

> Dallas, Texas
> September, 1976

At the Public Citizen Forum held in Washington, D.C., with Ralph Nader as moderator, Carter made the following opening remarks:

Thank you. First of all let me say that I am very pleased and proud to be here. To be sitting at the head table with such a distinguished group of courageous and

James Carter Jr

James Earl Carter Jr

(I use Jimmy Carter)

Jimmy Carter

effective Americans is an honor in itself. An accumulated talent, an ability and sensitivity and commitment of those who have just been introduced is, indeed, an inspiration to us all. The only one about whom I have any concern is our host, Ralph Nader. I was talking to Jack Brooks a few minutes ago and when Ralph's people went out to the audience to collect the question cards, Jack Brooks said, "I'm sure, knowing Nader, that he is taking up a collection." I said, "He is way ahead of that—he takes up a collection *before* you get in the house; he doesn't wait until you get in." I made the mistake of inviting Mr. Nader down to Plains this past weekend. I really wanted to make an impression on him because I have admired him so long, and in order to do so I took him out to the Plains softball field, and I was very pleased when Ralph and I got out of the car that all the tourists who now fill our tiny town rushed forward with their autograph books. I turned to get my pen out of my pocket. I then turned around to see all the tourists gathered around Mr. Nader instead of me. He brought, also, some bad luck. I have a seven-to-nothing record as a pitcher on the softball team on which I play. I lost my first game. In the midst of the game, my brother's gas station exploded; I wound up with two charly horses—one on each leg—and his performance as an umpire! I'd rather not comment on it.

He said that he was fair because both sides said he was lousy and I can't disagree with that.

I hope that this forum is not one of a series of catastrophes he has brought on me so far.

Washington, D.C.
August, 1976

Appearing before an audience during the Democratic Presidential race, Carter said:

I don't claim to be the man best qualified to be President of the United States. There are, right here in this room, people better qualified to be President than I am. And I want to thank you for not running this year: I've already got competition enough.

On Election Day, Carter walked out of the voting booth with a grin and said:

I voted for Walter Mondale *and* his running mate.

Plains, Georgia
November, 1976

After winning the Democratic Presidential nomination, Carter returned home. Hundreds of reporters and curious people surrounded his house. Amy, his daughter, set up a lemonade stand. Her father decided that the price of lemonade should be raised from five cents a glass to ten cents. Some of the reporters requested that they get a special discount. Carter said:

Reporters should pay double because they are on an expense account.

Plains, Georgia

21

Remarking on his first campaign for Governor of Georgia, Jimmy Carter said:

I was so unknown that some journalist labeled me "Jimmy Who."

On Labor Day Jimmy Carter spoke about the lack of leadership in the Ford White House and about scandals and mismanagement—with no one in authority admitting responsibility. Then he quipped:

Every time another ship runs aground—CIA, FBI, Panama, unemployment, deficits, welfare, inflation, Medicaid—the captain hides in his stateroom and the crew argues about who is to blame.

Warm Springs, Georgia
September, 1976

While Governor, Carter was appalled by Georgia's maze of three hundred overlapping state agencies. He recalled:

It had got so that every time I opened the door of my office, a new state agency would fall out.

At a reception at the Beverly Wilshire Hotel given by Warren Beatty, the actor, and attended by such guests as Peter Falk, Carroll O'Connor, and Faye Dunaway, Beatty remarked about the guests being "pinkos, leftists, commies." Carter retorted:

It is a real thrill to meet the famous people here tonight. I hope I don't get to know too much about you.

When Tony Randall said, "You've never met with people of this level," Carter quipped:
That's how I won the nomination.

Los Angeles, California
August, 1976

Campaigning through Mississippi for the Democratic Presidential nomination, he shook the hand of a manne-quin in a department store. He quickly pulled himself together and remarked:
Better give her a brochure too.

At a rally, Carter explained why there was such an age difference among his three grown sons and his youngest child, Amy:
My wife and I had an argument for fourteen years . . . which I finally won.

Warren, Rhode Island
May, 1976

During a speech at the Tristate Winter Conference, Carter said the following about his daughter, Amy:
She didn't learn to read until she was in the first grade about three months ago, and now she has read twenty-five books, and she feels that this is the most important thing in her life. Recently, there was a headline picture on the sports page of the Atlanta morning news-

paper with me as Governor representing the state and the legislators who were visiting the Atlanta Hawks Basketball game. And Amy was sitting in my lap reading a book and the title of the photograph was, "Did Winnie the Pooh Win?"

Georgia
February, 1974

At a press conference, Carter's opening remark was:
I'm glad to have you all here. I noticed the number of cars outside was two or three times larger than my total audience was a couple of years ago.

Plains, Georgia
November, 1976

Talking to reporters in Ohio on a press bus, Carter said:
You've treated me very well so far.
Compared to what?
To the way you treated Nixon.

June, 1976

24

At a mayors' conference, Carter said:

Dewey went around so long acting like he was President that the people thought it was time for a change. . . . I don't want that to happen to me.

Milwaukee, Wisconsin
June, 1976

When asked about his decision to get a tennis court and swimming pool for the Governor's mansion only a few weeks after he moved in, Carter said:

I need some place where I can relax. And actually I can think better at the bottom of a swimming pool than I can at some other places.

Atlanta, Georgia
May, 1971

During a speech addressed to the Georgia Association of Colleges, Jimmy Carter told the following story:

Early one morning immediately following my campaign, when I made my first foray into the rest of Georgia after becoming Governor, I went into a restaurant in southwest Georgia and I asked for an order of hotcakes and the girl in there brought me one little piece of butter. After I had finished about half the hotcakes, I called her over and told her that if she didn't mind I'd like to have some more butter. She turned around and walked away and said, "No." I figured she didn't understand what I meant, so the next time she came by, which was a quite a while later, I said, "Young lady, would you come over

25

here a minute, please; I'd like to have another pat of butter." And she said, "No," and she left again. Finally, I asked the security man who was with me to go get her and bring her back. When she walked over, I said, "Listen, I don't want to make an issue of this, but I want some more butter." She said, "You're not going to have it." And, I said, "Do you know who I am?" She said, "Who?" And I said, "I'm the Governor of Georgia." She said, "Do you know who I am?" I said, "No." She said, "I'm the keeper of the butter."

Athens, Georgia
August, 1973

Carter's sister, Ruth Carter Stapleton, complained about campaign exhaustion. Jimmy Carter replied:
Honey, I can will myself to sleep until ten thirty A.M. and get my ass beat, or I can will myself to get up at six A.M. and become President.

March, 1976

While giving a speech at a fundraiser, Carter said that he'd heard the answer-and-question bit done by Johnny Carson on the Tonight *show:*
The answer was: "Sixty minutes."
And the question was: "How long does it take Jimmy Carter to brush his teeth?"

Philadelphia, Pennsylvania
June, 1976

Carter stood before two thousand well-wishers, including astronaut Edwin (Buzz) Aldrin, and said:

As of this time here, in the state that I love, surrounded by friends of mine from all over the nation—in fact, even from the moon—I want to announce that I am a candidate for the Presidency of the United States.

Atlanta, Georgia
December, 1974

In a speech before an audience of Democrats, Carter said that a reporter had asked him how he would feel if his daughter had a premarital affair. His answer was:

I told him that Mrs. Carter and I would be deeply hurt and shocked and disappointed . . . because our daughter is only seven years old.

Naples, Florida
1975

Answering a question about extramarital affairs, Carter said at a senior citizens reception:

I think my wife . . . is sure of my loyalty. . . . She knows how hard I work. She knows how tired I am every night. She knows I have fifty or sixty reporters watching me day and night.

Long Beach, California
June, 1976

27

Speaking before the United Rubber Workers Union, Carter was asked, "Who is your favorite Vice President?" Carter answered:

Harry Truman.

After the laughter subsided, he said he was sorry for making fun of the question. He continued:

I know what you mean. But I think it would be presumptuous of me to start naming Vice Presidents when I haven't even got a nomination yet.

During the Iowa primary, Carter on occasion would have two staff members help him. Carter and two of his aides, Jody Powell and Greg Schneiders, arrived at an airstrip early one morning. Carter and Schneiders boarded the plane and as it taxied down the runway, Schneiders reminded Carter that Powell was not on board. Schneiders asked the pilot to radio the terminal and discovered that Powell was inside using the telephone. A few minutes later, Powell raced out of the terminal, caught up with the waiting plane, and climbed inside. Carter, who had been willing to take off without his press secretary, said:

Jody, you've got one friend on this airplane—and it ain't me.

Speaking before a Jefferson-Jackson Day fundraising dinner, Carter told the following story:

We have every Sunday morning at our church a large number of people who come now to visit—I started to say

28

worship with us. Some of them apparently haven't been in church very often, but we always make room for them and welcome them there. A couple of Sundays ago, there were two tourists from Miami who left the church after the service, and one of them turned to the other and said, "How did I do in the service?" And the other fellow said, "Well, you did O.K., but the word is *Hallelujah* and not *Hialeah*."

Charleston, West Virginia

Speaking before an audience in New York, Carter said:
If all the things the Republicans are saying about me are true, I wouldn't vote for myself either.

New York City
October, 1976

During his first gubernatorial campaign, Carter said to an audience:
During this campaign you may well ask, "Jimmy Who?" about my last name, but you will never have to ask, "Jimmy What?" about my last book or my last radio or TV appearance.

In his speech at the Alfred E. Smith Memorial dinner, Carter compared himself to the former New York Governor and identified himself with New York City, of which Smith was a native, by saying:

We must say to New York City not drop dead but stay alive, hang on, help is on the way—together we will live forever.

New York City
October, 1976

Speaking before an audience in New York, Carter referred to an interview he had given to Playboy *on the topic of lust:*

If I ever give another interview on the biblical sins of pride and lust, it will be to the reporter from *Our Sunday Visitor* [a Catholic weekly newspaper].

New York City
October, 1976

Jimmy Carter, during a speech, commented on campaigning:

I have made my share of mistakes. If any of my supporters began this campaign believing I was infallible, I think I have by now disabused them of that notion.

But that is as it should be. The American people should see the Presidential candidate warts and all. We've had enough slickly packaged candidates. We should cast our vote for real people, not for images.

New York City
October, 1976

Speaking before an audience at the Alfred E. Smith Dinner, Carter said:

One of the concerns we share, and that Al Smith shared, is for our cities. Al Smith was a child of the city. The Lower East Side was his kindergarten, and he once told a Cornell man that his alma mater was FFM—the Fulton Fish Market.

New York City
October, 1976

31

Growing Up

Carter wrote about his black boyhood friends:

We hunted, fished, explored, worked, and slept together. We ground sugar cane, plowed mules, pruned watermelons, dug and bedded sweet potatoes, mopped cotton, stacked peanuts, cut stovewood, pumped water, fixed fences, fed chickens, picked velvet beans, and hauled cotton to the gin together.

In addition to many chores, we also found time to spend the night on the banks of Choctawhatchee and Kinchafoonee creeks, catching and cooking catfish and eels when the water was rising from heavy rains.

We ran, swam, rode horse, drove wagons, and floated on rafts together. We misbehaved together and shared the same punishments. We built and lived in the same tree houses and played cards and ate at the same table.

But we never went to the same church or school. Our social life and our church life were strictly separate. We did not sit together on the two-car diesel train that could be flagged down in Archery. There was a scrupulous compliance with these unwritten and unspoken rules. I never heard them questioned. Not then.

October, 1975

35

When Carter was at the United States Naval Academy, he wrote in his diary about what makes Georgia boys different from the others:

Bowen came around tonight and talked about the cruise and women, mostly women, as do all the other Ga. boys. Joe said that's the way he recognizes them.

Annapolis, Maryland

While at the Naval Academy, a third classman started to lean on Carter, trying to make him sing the Yankee battle song made famous by Sherman, "Marching Through Georgia." Carter rebelled and wrote in his diary:

Weidner is kinda mad at me now. He said—"Learn Marching Thru Ga." 3 times and I said, "Sir?" every time. He was pretty mad and yelled it again and told me not to say "sir?" again. He really got mad when I said "aye, aye" with no "sir." Told me to come around, but I haven't been yet.

Annapolis, Maryland

When Jimmy Carter was twelve years old, he put together a document entitled "Jimmy Carter's Health Report." In it he wrote:

The healthy boy is clean. Teeth, the skin, hair, hands and the mind should be kept clean. . . . Teeth should be kept clean because clean teeth help your looks, health and helps to keep a good digestive system. . . . To look good one must have the skin clean. The skin is very im-

36

The train station in Plains from which candidate Carter addressed campaign and victory rallies.

portant because the skin can have many diseases, itch, hives, heat and many other things.

A clean skin is entitled to clean clothes. . . . Your head does not like a tight hat nor your feet tight shoes. . . . Frequently take a good hot bath. Bathing gets rid of germs. A clean mouth is necessary. . . . Breathe through the nose and not through the mouth.

Plains, Georgia
1936

In a section called "Healthy Mental Habits," he wrote:
There are certain habits of thinking which have a good effect upon health. If you think in the right way, you'll develop.

1. The habit of expecting to accomplish what you attempt.

2. The habit of expecting to like other people and to have them like you.

3. The habit of deciding quickly what you want to do, and doing it.

4. The habit of "sticking to it."

5. The habit of welcoming fearlessly all wholesome ideas and experiences.

6. A person who wants to build good mental habits should avoid the idle daydream; should give up worry and anger, hatred and envy; should neither fear nor be ashamed of anything that is honest or purposeful.

Plains, Georgia
1936

Jimmy Carter wrote in his diary when he was a nineteen-year-old plebe at the Naval Academy:

Of course all of the plebes were rather apprehensive about what was to come. We later found out that our fears were well-grounded. The first night after supper the halls were lined with youngsters who were anxious to try out their new authority. . . . We had to tell our names and home state to every youngster we saw. . . . My main trouble was that I smiled too much. I soon learned to concentrate on a serious subject when passing a group of the yapping 3/C. I also learned how to "wipe it off."

Annapolis, Maryland

In a speech before the Cleveland City Club, Carter spoke about the book War and Peace *and what it meant to him as a boy:*

I remember that I started reading books as an isolated country boy when I was very young. I had a superintendent, named Miss Julia Coleman, who encouraged me to do so. One of the first books that she recommended to me, after I had finished a list of classical volumes, was *War and Peace*. She used to give a silver star for every five books, a gold star for every ten, and finally said, "Jimmy, I think you're ready now"—I was about twelve years old—"to read *War and Peace*." And I breathed a sigh of relief because, after all those classical books, I thought I was finally going to read something about cowboys and Indians; but when I went to the library and checked the book out, I was stricken because it was 1,450 pages thick.

But that book I've read several times since then; and, as you know, it is a story about Napoleon who went into Russia, hoping to be the conqueror of the world, completely confident. But he underestimated two things: the love of the peasant for his land and the severity of the Russian winter. And to make a long story short, he retreated in defeat. Then the course of human events were changed. And the book is not about Napoleon or the Czar of Russia. It is about the common, ordinary people—barbers, housewives, privates in the Army, farmers, and others—and the point that Tolstoy makes is that the course of human events, even the greatest historical events, are controlled and shaped, not by the leaders of the nations, but by the combined hopes and dreams and aspirations and courage and convictions of the common, ordinary people. And if that's true in a nation like Russia with a Czar or France with an Emperor, how much more true it is in our own country; for under the Constitution of the United States, we are guaranteed, not only the right, but the duty, to let our own individual aspirations, trust, moral judgment, character, shape our government. I believe we have a nation that will respond to that kind of public sentiment and public involvement.

Cleveland, Ohio
April, 1976

Speaking before an audience, Carter told the following story:
    I remember when I was a child, I lived on a farm about three miles from Plains, and we didn't have elec-

tricity or running water. We lived on the railroad—Seaboard Coastline railroad. Like all farm boys I had a flip, a slingshot. They had stabilized the railroad bed with little white round rocks, which I used for ammunition. I would go out frequently to the railroad and gather the most perfectly shaped rocks of proper size. I always had a few in my pockets, and I had others cached away around the farm, so that they would be convenient if I ran out of my pocket supply.

One day I was leaving the railroad track with my pockets full of rocks and hands full of rocks, and my mother came out on the front porch—this is not a very interesting story, but it illustrates a point—and she had in her hands a plate full of cookies that she had just baked for me. She called me, I am sure with love in her heart, and said, "Jimmy, I've baked some cookies for you." I remember very distinctly walking up to her and standing there for fifteen or twenty seconds, in honest doubt about whether I should drop those rocks which were worthless and take the cookies that my mother had prepared for me, which between her and me were very valuable.

Athens, Georgia
May, 1974

41

Rosalynn, Miss Lillian, Billy, Amy: The Carter Family

Carter talked about his wife, Rosalynn, in the famous
Playboy *interview:*

Well, I really love Rosalynn more now than I did when I first married her. And I have loved no other woman except her. I had gone out with all kinds of girls, sometimes fairly steadily, but I just never cared about them. Rosalynn had been a friend of my sister's and was three years younger than I, which is a tremendous chasm in the high school years. She was just one of those insignificant little girls around the house. Then, when I was twenty-one, and home from the Navy on leave, I took her to the movies. Nothing extraordinary happened, but the next morning I told my mother, "That's the girl I want to marry." It's the best thing that ever happened to me.

We also share a religious faith, and the two or three times in our married life when we've had a serious crisis, I think that's what sustained our marriage and helped us overcome our difficulty. Our children, too, have been a

45

factor binding Rosalynn and me together. After the boys, Amy came along late and it's been especially delightful for me, maybe because she's a little girl.

Plains, Georgia
November, 1976

Carter wrote about his mother:
    As the matriarch of our family, my mother, Lillian, provided a nucleus around which our different individual families revolved. She is an extrovert, very dynamic, inquisitive in her attitude about life, compassionate toward others, and has had a wide variety of experiences in her advancing years.

October, 1975

Jimmy Carter wrote the following about his daughter, Amy:
    Amy was three years old when we moved into the governor's mansion in early 1971, and she has had a rapidly developing life among adults. She is probably the most famous member of our family, being interviewed and photographed continually at a young age and being actively involved in all sorts of state actvities.

October, 1975

46

The Carters have a brief encounter in Cleveland during the Presidential campaign. Rep. Louis Stokes and Sen. John Glenn look on.

In a TV interview, Jimmy Carter talked about his father:
If all the other field workers were off for the afternoon, and he wanted me to turn the potato vine so they could be plowed Monday morning, Daddy would say to me, "Hot"—"Hot Shot" is what he called me. He says, "Hot, would you like to turn the potato vines this afternoon?" And I would much rather go to the movie or something. But I always said, "Yes, sir, Daddy, I would." And I would do it. But he didn't have to give me many direct orders. But I never did disobey a direct order my father gave me.

May, 1976

Jimmy Carter described his youngest brother, Billy:
My brother, Billy, reminds me of my father—in appearance, habits and attitudes. When we returned home from the Navy, Billy was only sixteen years old, and not at all inclined to take orders from an older brother. As soon as he finished high school, he left to join the Marine Corps and shortly thereafter married his childhood sweetheart, Sybil Spires. A few years later they came back home to live, Billy became a partner in our business, and now he runs it in my absence. Our friendship has grown steadily with the years, and I realize that his willingness to operate our farms and warehouse has made it possible for me to hold public office.

October, 1975

Carter wrote about his father in Atlanta *magazine:*

I came from the Navy to see my daddy die and the thought struck me that here were my roots, here were my ancestors, these were the fields I had worked in, these are the people I grew up with. . . . I felt that my daddy's life meant more, in the long run, than mine had meant, so I got out of the Navy.

During an interview, Carter was asked what people touched him the most. He answered:

Mother always was a champion of disadvantaged people. In our area it was poor whites and all blacks. Later, when she was past retirement age, she, as you know, went to India for two years, and she came back when she was past seventy. She was in the Peace Corps.

May, 1976

In a TV interview, Carter discussed obedience:

Well, as a matter of fact, I never disobeyed my father in that when he said, "Jimmy, you do something," I never failed to do it. But on many occasions I did things that I knew my father didn't like, and I was punished very severely because of it. In fact, my father very seldom gave me an order. If all the other field workers were off for the afternoon, and he wanted me to turn the potato vines so they could be plowed Monday morning, Daddy would say to me—he called me "Hot" [short for "Hot Shot"]—"Hot,

49

would you like to turn the potato vines this afternoon?"
And I would much rather go to the movies or something,
but I always said, "Yes, sir, daddy, I would." And I would
do it. But he didn't have to give me many direct orders,
but I never did disobey a direct order . . . it wasn't a
namby-pamby sort of thing. My father was my friend and
I respected him. I never said, "Yes," or "No," to my father.
I'd say, "Yes, sir," or "No, sir." To my mother, too. Still
do. And to most people I don't know well. But it was a
matter of respect. It wasn't any matter of trying to kow-
tow to him.

May, 1976

*Jimmy Carter explained why he left the Navy to go back
to live in his home town in Plains, Georgia:*
I worked for Rickover until 1953, when my father
died of cancer. I was permitted to go home on leave
during his terminal illness, and I spent hours by his bed-
side. We talked about old times together and about
those intervening eleven years when we had rarely seen
each other. . . . Hundreds of people came by to speak
to daddy, or to bring him a choice morsel of food or
some fresh flowers. It was obvious that he meant much
to them, and it caused me to compare my life perspective
with his. After his funeral, I went back to Schenectady.
. . . I began to think about the relative significance of
his life and mine. He was an integral part of the community, and had a wide range of varied but interrelated
interests and responsibilities. He was his own boss, and

his life was stabilized by slow and evolutionary changes in the local societal structure. . . . After some torturous days, I decided to resign from the Navy and to come home to Plains—to a tiny town, a church, a farm, and uncertain income.

October, 1975

In a speech before an audience at the Martin Luther King hospital, Carter said of his mother:

My mother was a registered nurse. She would work twelve hours a day or twenty hours a day and then come home and care for her family and minister to the people of our little community, both black and white.

My mother knew no color line. Her black friends were just as welcome in our home as her white friends, a fact that shocked some people, sometimes even my father, who was very conventional then in his views on race.

Los Angeles, California
June, 1976

Appearing before the National Education Association, Carter said:

Our intention is that when Amy comes to Washington she'll be in the public schools and if there are problems there I want to be part of the solution of those problems. This is a national commitment that ought to be dramatized. We do have problems in education, but they are not problems that ought to be permanent with us. And if a nation like Sweden or a nation like Israel can achieve almost universal literacy, I see no reason why that is too high a standard to set in our great country.

Washington, D.C.
September, 1976

I Believe . . .

Jimmy Carter told the following story during an interview on television:

I was going through a state in my life that was a very difficult one. I had run for Governor and lost. Everything I did was not gratifying. When I succeeded in something, it was a horrible experience for me. And I thought I was a good Christian. I was the Chairman of the Board of Deacons. I was the head of the Brotherhood in all the thirty-four churches in my district, and head of the Finance Committee, and Sunday School teacher just about all my life. I thought I was a great Christian.

And one day the preacher gave the sermon—I don't remember a thing he said—I just remember the title which you described—"If you were arrested for being a Christian, would there be any evidence to convict you?"

And my answer by the time that sermon was over was "No." I never had really committed myself totally to God—my Christian beliefs were superficial. Based primarily on pride, and—I'd never done much for other people. I was always thinking about myself, and I changed

55

somewhat for the better. I formed a much more intimate relationship with Christ. And since then, I've had just about like a new life. As far as hatreds, frustrations, I feel at ease with myself. And it doesn't mean that I'm better, but I'm better off myself.

May, 1976

During an interview for a magazine, Carter talked about his faith:

Belief in the forgiveness of God gives me the freedom to take chances and make mistakes. . . . I feel contention with God at times—why is there suffering and doubt and death and hunger?—but even the struggle is contributing to a deeper sense of assurance. The alternative is a belief in permanent death.

Plains, Georgia
November, 1976

During a speech, Carter commented on the law and the Christian ethic:

I am a Sunday school teacher, and I've always known that the structure of law is founded on the Christian ethic that you shall love the Lord your God and your neighbor as yourself—a very high and perfect standard. We all know [that] the fallibility of man, and the contentions in society, as described by Reinhold Neibuhr and many others, don't permit us to achieve perfection.

Athens, Georgia
May, 1974

Greeting friends after church in Plains.

In an interview, Carter discussed civil law and God's law:
I say judge not that ye be not judged. For example, adultery or homosexuals. God taught us to obey civil law and authority. We must reach compatibility between civil and God's law. If there is disharmony, obey God's law, but accept punishment. Governments have been evolved subsequent to religious construction. Worship first, then civil government, then attempt to make the two compatible.

Plains, Georgia
November, 1976

Carter, explaining himself during a TV interview, said:
But, as you know, Christians don't have a monopoly on the truth, and when I go out of office, if I'm elected, at the end of four years or eight years, I hope people will say, "You know, Jimmy Carter made a lot of mistakes, but he never told me a lie."

May, 1976

Carter discussed the possibility of assassination while he was running for President in a magazine interview:
I just look at death as not a threat. It's inevitable, and I have an assurance of eternal life. . . . I don't say that in a mysterious way; I recognize the possibility of assassination. . . . But I just don't worry.

Plains, Georgia
November, 1976

In a magazine interview, Jimmy Carter caused quite a stir by saying the following with regard to adultery:

I try not to commit a deliberate sin. I recognize that I'm going to do it anyway, because I am human and I'm tempted. And Christ sets some almost impossible standards for us. Christ said, "I tell you that anyone who looks on a woman with lust has in his heart already committed adultery."

I've looked on a lot of women with lust. I've committed adultery in my heart many times. This is something that God recognizes I will do—and I have done it—and God forgives me for it. But that doesn't mean that I condemn someone who not only looks on a woman with lust but who leaves his wife and shacks up with someone out of wedlock.

God says, don't consider yourself better than someone else because one guy screws a whole bunch of women while the other guy is loyal to his wife. The guy who's loyal to his wife ought not to be condescending or proud because of the relative degree of sinfulness.

Plains, Georgia
November, 1976

During an interview Carter was asked, "Have you ever felt lust?" He answered:

Oh, yes, but I feel terribly sinful about it when I do. And the same with an eye for an eye and a tooth for a tooth. Don't be proud of your behavior if you've ever looked on your brother with hatred or thought someone a fool. I feel bad about the things I have said about

Hubert Humphrey and Mo Udall. In politics you're always caught up in combat, politically speaking. You receive a report in the course of the campaign emphasizing your opponent's comments, and there's no way to call him before speaking in response.

Yes, I wish I hadn't said and thought the things I did. For the most difficult thing in my life is to admit lust, anger, and hatred. But when I talk with God I can't say simply and vaguely, "Forgive me *all* my sins." I must spell them out, and that hurts. So I tell Him I was lusting after someone else or grasping for advantage or derogating an opponent. And then belief in the forgiveness of God gives me a deep security, confidence, and independence from everyday concerns.

Plains, Georgia
November, 1976

During a TV interview Carter was asked, "What do you think we're on earth for?" He replied:
I don't know. I could quote the biblical references to creation, that God created us in His own image, hoping that we'd be perfect, and we turned out to be not perfect but very sinful. And then when Christ was asked what are the two great Commandments from God which should direct our lives, he said, "To love God with all your heart and soul and mind, and love your neighbor as yourself." So I try to take that condensation of the Christian theology and let it be something through which I search for a meaningful existence. I don't worry about it too much any more. I used to when I was a college sophomore, and

we used to debate for hours and hours about why we're here, who made us, where shall we go, what's our purpose.

But I don't feel frustrated about it. You know, I'm not afraid to see my life ended. I feel like every day is meaningful. I don't have any fear at all of death. I feel like I'm doing the best I can, and if I get elected President, I'll have a chance to magnify my own influence, maybe for—in a meaningful way. If I don't get elected President, I'll go back to Plains. So I feel like a sense of equanimity about it. But what—why we're here on earth, I don't know. I'd like to hear your views on the subject.

May, 1976

When he became Governor of Georgia, Jimmy Carter said:

I see every legitimate concern of government as a legitimate concern of Christians. I have considered myself in "full-time Christian service" every day I have been Governor.

At a news conference while running for the Democratic Presidential nomination, Carter was asked if he believed that everything in the Bible was literally true. He responded:

I don't believe everything in the Bible to be literally true. I don't think the earth was created in seven days as we know days now and I reserve the right to make my own interpretation.

61

While pursuing the Democratic Presidential nomination, Carter said to a predominantly Jewish audience of two thousand:

I worship the same God you do; we [Baptists] study the same Bible that you do. This is a country wherein one's own religious faith should not be a matter of prejudice or concern. The ability of Jews, Catholics, Baptists, even atheists to work in harmony with one another in our nation, based on a system of religious pluralism, is one that is precious to me.

Elizabeth, New Jersey
June, 1976

Three days after accepting the Democratic Presidential nomination, Jimmy Carter stood before his adult Sunday School class in Plains. He began with the biblical quotation "God is love." He said to his class:

As I put it in my acceptance speech the other night, out of love must come one more thing. Does anyone remember?

One man responded, "Obedience." Carter said:

Simple justice. . . . Who was Christ with?

A class member answered, "Sinners." Carter said:

Yes. And prostitutes, cheaters, tax collectors, the common people, the dark-skinned people. The average person with whom Christ lived would not speak to those of a different color or religion. Do we do the same thing? [He and his family, more than fifteen years ago, had tried to integrate the church he was speaking in.]

Quite often, if we go into a Baptist church in the

South, there's a social and economic élite. We're the prominent people in the town. There's a tendency to think that because I've been accepted by God, I'm better than other people.

One thing I wish the Southern Baptist Church did— as the Primitive Baptist do—is the washing of feet, one of the most moving Christian experiences. . . .

This is what you need to remember: let us love one another. As Dr. Martin Luther King, Sr., said the other night, if you have got any hatred left in your heart, get down on your knees. . . .

You do not have to have a preacher. You do not even have to have a Sunday School teacher. You just have to have a simple faith.

Plains, Georgia
July, 1976

Governor Carter, speaking before the Youth for Christ of Metropolitan Atlanta, said:
Jesus Christ is the most important factor in my life. I rely on Him and intense prayer. . . .

I'm a politician and I'm a Christian, and I see no conflict.

After all the purpose of politics is to establish justice in a sinful world. I spend much time in prayer on my knees in the back room of the Governor's office.

Atlanta, Georgia
May, 1972

63

While speaking before a church congregation, Carter said:
I believe I can be a better President because of my faith. I did not ask God "Let me succed" but, "Let me do the right thing."

Buffalo, New York
Spring, 1976

At a press conference, Carter explained that he did not have a Messiah complex. He said:
I don't think God is going to make me President by any means. But whatever I have as a responsibility for the rest of my life, it will be with that infinite personal continuing relationship.

April, 1976

During the last day of campaigning in New York for the Presidential nomination, Jimmy Carter said of his religious convictions:
When the media began to emphasize my beliefs, I did not know how to deal with it: whether to answer the questions or say I didn't have a comment.

I decided to tell the truth, not to conceal it but reveal it. If there are those who don't want to vote for me because I'm a deeply committed Christian, I believe they should vote for someone else.

Carter vows a strict separation of church and state and denies there is any conflict between the two. He said:

The Bible says, "Render unto Caesar the things which are Caesar's and unto God the things that are God's." It doesn't say you have to live two lives. It doesn't say you have to be two people. [My religious convictions] will make me a better President.

The Bible is Jimmy Carter's prime source of belief—but he reads it somewhat critically. He said the following:

I find it difficult to question Holy Scriptures, but I admit that I do have trouble with Paul sometimes, especially when he says that a woman's place is with her husband, and that she should keep quiet and cover her head in church. I just can't go along with him on that.

In an interview for a magazine, Carter said:

As Christ became my friend, other lives began meaning more to me. I became less proud and stopped judging others all the time. I ran once again for Governor and knew that whether I won or lost, I could approach the result with complete equanimity. And though my term as Governor was tough and combative and contentious, the day we drove from the Governor's mansion I told my wife I'd never gotten up on a single morning without looking forward to the day with great anticipation. For unlike Lyndon Johnson . . . I feel sure about myself deep inside. Johnson never felt secure inside, especially around the Eastern Establishment—the professor, experts, writers, and media people—and that's why they got him in the end. But I don't feel ill-at-ease in a Harvard professor's house, or when I'm talking with experts on foreign policy or on economics, or when I'm with the leader of any group.

The point is that I'm not comparing myself with any of them. To judge our own goodness or sinfulness by comparison with other men is wrong. We all fall short in comparison with the glory of Christ. The Bible says, "Thou shalt not commit adultery." But I'm never proud of simply not sleeping with someone else. For if you've ever looked with lust upon another woman, you're equally guilty. Pride comes only when such sinful thoughts can be abolished.

Plains, Georgia
November, 1976

In an interview, Carter talked about being "born again":
I was quoted as saying I was "twice born," but the expression I use is "born again." We believe that the first time we're born as children, it's human life given to us; and when we accept Jesus as our Saviour it's a new life. That's what "born again" means. I was baptized when I was eleven years old. I never did have a personal feeling of intimacy with Christ until, I'd say, ten, twelve years ago, and then I began to see much more clearly the significance of Christ in my life, and it changed my attitudes drastically. . . .

I became much more deeply committed to study and using my example to explain to other people about Christ. I did a lot of missionary work.

Carter was then asked how his religious beliefs guide him in his political career. He replied:

It has no particular political significance. It's something that's with me every day.

Washington, D.C.
March, 1976

Jimmy Carter spoke at a press conference about his profound religious experience of seeing the light, which occurred when he began to make plans to run for Governor of Georgia in 1970:

I realized that my own relationship with God, with Christ, was very superficial. And because of some experiences I had that I won't describe involving personal witnessing in states outside Georgia among people who were very unfortunate and who did not speak English and otherwise, I came to realize that my Christian life, which I had always professed to be preeminent, had really been a secondary interest in my life.

I formed a very close, intimate personal relationship with God, through Christ, that has given me a great deal of peace, equanimity, and the ability to accept difficulty without unnecessarily being disturbed. . . .

It was not a profound stroke, a miracle, it wasn't a voice of God from Heaven. It was not anything of that kind. It wasn't mysterious.

It might have been the same kind of experience as millions of people have who become Christians in a deeply personal way. . . .

67

I don't think God is going to make me President by any means. But whatever I have as a responsibility for the rest of my life, it will be with that intimate, personal, continuing relationship.

Washington, D.C.
1976

After Carter had lost his first campaign for Governor of Georgia, he said to his sister, Ruth Stapleton:
I want the fullness of Christ in my life more than I want anything—even politics. . . . I would really rather have the fullness of Christ in my life than be President.

Plains, Georgia
1966

Civil Rights

Four months after taking office as Governor of Georgia, Jimmy Carter said:

I know my people; and I am saying what they are thinking. The people of Georgia have been through periods of great crisis. My generation has had to assimilate many changes. Our black and white citizens have decided there will be no more restraint on their search to work together. Our problem and our opportunities are completely mutual. We have a lot of problems left concerning race, but we are no longer preoccupied with this problem to the exclusion of others. There is a new dynamic, a new freedom that exists throughout the South.

Atlanta, Georgia

Commenting on his southern roots, Carter said:

I do have unique experience and one of the strongest and best of these is my relationship with poor people. That's where I come from. That's where I live. Those are my people—not only whites, but particularly blacks.

July, 1976

Carter, a strong advocate of civil rights, has said:

The passage of the civil rights acts during the 1960s was the greatest thing to happen to the South in my lifetime. It lifted a burden from the whites as well as the blacks.

Carter, in his inaugural address as Governor of Georgia said:

At the end of a long campaign, I believe I know the people of this state as well as anyone. Based on this knowledge of Georgians North and South, rural and urban, liberal and conservative, I say to you quite frankly that the time for racial discrimination is over.

Our people have already made this major and difficult decision, but we cannot underestimate the challenge of hundreds of minor decisions yet to be made.

Our inherent human charity and our religious beliefs will be taxed to the limit. No poor, rural, weak, or black person should ever have to bear the additional burden of being deprived of the opportunity of an education, a job, or simple justice.

Atlanta, Georgia
January, 1971

In response to an attempt by several deacons of churches in Americus, Georgia, to vote against allowing blacks to attend services, Carter said:

I can't have this vote taken until I explain my views. . . . When my father died, the back of the church was

A hug and a kiss from his mother, Miss Lillian, after he announced his candidacy for the presidency.

full of blacks who lived on the farm and who loved my father. This is not my house; this is not your house. I believe that I can keep anyone out of my house that I want, and you can. But I for one will never stand in the doors of this church and keep anyone out.

The racially segregated community Carter came from as a boy is illustrated in the following story. It was during a fight between Joe Louis and Max Schmeling that black neighbors of the Carters asked to hear the fight on the Carter's radio. Joe Louis won the fight. According to Carter, their black neighbors reacted as follows:

There was no sound from anyone in the yard except a polite, "Thank you, Mr. Earl," offered to my father.

Then our several dozen visitors filed across the dirt road across the railroad track, and quietly entered a house about a hundred yards away out in the field. At that point, pandemonium broke loose inside the house, as our black neighbors shouted and yelled in celebration of the Louis victory. But all the curious accepted proprieties of a racially segregated society had been carefully observed.

During a speech, Carter said of Martin Luther King, Jr:

Dr. Martin Luther King, Jr., who was perhaps despised by many in this room because he shook up our social structure that benefited us, and demanded simply that black citizens be treated the same as white citizens, wasn't greeted with approbation and accolades by the Georgia Bar Association or the Alabama Bar Association. He was greeted with horror. Still, once that change was made, a very simple but difficult change, no one in his right mind would want to go back to circumstances prior to that juncture in the development of our nation's society.

Athens, Georgia
May, 1974

Carter explained in an interview the "unique experience" that he believed he would bring to the White House:
One of the strongest and best of these [experiences] is my relationship with poor people. That's what I came from. That's where I lived. Those are my people—not only whites, but particularly blacks—and it's not an accident that Andy Young and Daddy King support me. They know that I understand their problems. They know that I've demonstrated an eagerness to solve them, and I think the strength of this country in the future is dependent on that.

New York City
June, 1976

Jimmy Carter reminisced about his days in the Georgia senate:
The first speech I ever made in the Georgia senate, representing the most conservative district in Georgia, was concerning the abolition of thirty questions that we had so proudly evoked as a subterfuge to keep black citizens from voting and which we used with a great deal

of smirking and pride for decades or generations ever since the War Between the States—questions that nobody could answer in this room, but which were applied to every black citizen that came to the Sumter County Courthouse or Webster County Courthouse and said, "I want to vote." I spoke in that chamber, fearful of the news media reporting it back home, but overwhelmed with a commitment to the abolition of the artificial barrier to the rights of an American citizen. I remember the thing that I used in my speech, that a black pencil salesman on the outer door of the Sumter County Courthouse could make a better judgment about who ought to be sheriff than two highly educated professors at Georgia Southwestern College.

From the
Governor's Mansion

In his inaugural address as Governor of Georgia in 1970, Carter said:

[The test of government] . . . is not how popular it is among the powerful and privileged few, but how honestly and fairly it deals with the many who must depend upon it.

Atlanta, Georgia
January, 1971

After taking office as Governor of Georgia, Carter had the following to say about his undertaking:

Government at all levels can be competent, economical, and efficient. Yet I would hasten to point out that nowhere in the Constitution of the United States, or the Declaration of Independence, or the Bill of Rights, or the Emancipation Proclamation, or the Old Testament, or the New Testament, do you find the words *economy* or *efficiency*. Not that these two words are unimportant.

79

But you discover other words like honesty, integrity, fairness, liberty, justice, courage, patriotism, compassion, love —and many others which describe the qualities that a human being ought to possess. These are also the same words which describe the qualities that a government of human beings ought to possess.

When running for Governor of Georgia again, after losing in 1966, Carter said:
I remembered the admonition, "You show me a good loser and I will show you a loser." I did not intend to lose again.

When beginning to launch his candidacy, Carter said:
There is no clear vision of what is to be accomplished. Everyone struggles for temporary advantage, and there is no way to monitor how effectively services are delivered.

In his gubernatorial inauguration address, Carter said:
It is a long way from Plains to Atlanta. I started the trip four and a half years ago and, with a four-year detour, I finally made it. I thank you all for making it possible for me to be here on what is certainly the greatest day of my life. But now the election is over, and I realize the test of a man is not how well he campaigned, but how effectively he meets the challenges and responsibilities of office.

Atlanta, Georgia
January, 1971

The Carters dance at his 1971 Governor's Inaugural Ball.

As Governor of Georgia, in a speech he gave at Emory University, Carter talked about how the South was misunderstood:

One of the great afflictions on the South in the past . . . is that . . . politicians have underestimated the southern people. This has caused lack of . . . accurate analysis of the quality of the South . . . by the rest of the nation and the world.

Atlanta, Georgia

Carter said in his inaugural address as Governor of Georgia:

I am determined that at the end of this administration we shall be able to stand up anywhere in the world—in New York, California, or Florida—and say "I'm a Georgian"—and be proud of it.

I welcome the challenge and the opportunity of serving as Governor of our state during the next four years. I promise you my best. I ask you for your best.

Atlanta, Georgia
January, 1971

Carter said of the 1970 gubernatorial campaign:

Georgians are conservatives, and I told them that conservatism and racism are not the same thing. We talked about the positive aspects of conservatism: the opposition to big government, the flag, patriotism. We made that pitch hundreds of times. This gave me a rapport with the voters, and it did not remind them or make them think of past deficiencies.

At the end of his inaugural address as Governor of Georgia, Jimmy Carter said:

In a democracy, no government can be stronger, or wiser, or more just, than its people. The idealism of the college student, the compassion of a mother, the common sense of the businessman, the time and experience of a retired couple, and the vision of political leaders must all be harnessed to bring out the best in our state.

As I have said many times during the last few years, I am determined that at the end of this administration we shall be able to stand up anywhere in the world—in New York, California, or Florida—and say, "I'm a Georgian"—and be proud of it.

Atlanta, Georgia
January, 1971

In a speech as Governor of Georgia, Carter said:

Our people are our most precious possession and we cannot afford to waste the talents and abilities given by God to one single Georgian. Every adult illiterate, every school dropout, every untrained retarded child is an indictment of us all. Our state pays a terrible and continuing human financial price for these failures. It is time to end this waste. If Switzerland and Israel and other people can eliminate illiteracy, then so can we. The responsibility is our own, and as Governor, I will not shirk this responsibility.

Atlanta, Georgia
January, 1976

In a magazine article, Carter wrote:
I do believe that being from a rural community has helped me politically and has given me the assurance that there is no inherent difference between the problems [and opportunities] of urban and rural Georgians.

Governor Carter cited an example of injustice in a speech given at the University of Georgia:
I was in the Governor's mansion for two years, enjoying the services of a very fine cook, who was a prisoner —a woman. One day she came to me, after she got over her two years of timidity, and said, "Governor, I would like to borrow $250.00 from you."

I said, "I'm not sure that a lawyer would be worth that much."

She said, "I don't want to hire a lawyer; I want to pay the judge."

I thought it was a ridiculous statement for her; I felt that she was ignorant. But I found out she wasn't. She had been sentenced by a Superior Court judge in the state, who still serves, to seven years or $750. She had raised, early in her prison career, $500. I didn't lend her the money, but I had Bill Harper, my legal aide, look into it. He found the circumstances were true. She was quickly released under a court ruling that had come down in the last few years.

Atlanta, Georgia
May, 1974

In a speech, Governor Carter discussed prisons:
As a farmer, I'm not qualified to assess the characteristics of the 9,100 inmates in the Georgia prisons, fifty percent of whom ought not to be there. They ought to be on probation or under some other supervision . . . I don't know, it may be that poor people are the only ones who commit crimes, but I do know that they are the only ones who serve prison sentences.

Atlanta, Georgia
May, 1974

As Governor of Georgia, Carter talked about the criminal justice system:
My own interest in the criminal justice system is very deep and heartfelt. Not having studied law, I've had to learn the hard way. I read a lot and listen a lot. One of the sources for my understanding about the proper application of criminal justice and the system of equality is from reading Reinhold Niebuhr. . . . The other source of my understanding about what's right and wrong in this society is from a friend of mine, a poet named Bob Dylan.

85

After listening to his records about "The Ballad of Hattie Carol" and "Like a Rolling Stone" and "The Times They Are A-Changing," I've learned to appreciate the dynamism of change in a modern society.

I grew up as a landowner's son. But I don't think I ever realized the proper interrelationship between the landowner and those who worked on a farm until I heard Dylan's record, "I Ain't Gonna Work on Maggie's Farm No More." So I come here speaking to you today about your subject with a base for my information founded on Reinhold Niebuhr and Bob Dylan.

Atlanta, Georgia
May, 1974

Seeking the
Presidential Nomination

Jimmy Carter wrote about his strategy when he first began to campaign for the Democratic Presidential nomination:

Our strategy was simple: make a total effort all over the nation. After leaving office as governor, during the first months alone, I visited more than half the states, some of them several times. Each visit was carefully planned—by my small Atlanta staff and a local volunteer in each community—to be included during the week's trip. Our purposes during this early stage of the campaign were: to become known among those who have a continuing interest in politics and government; to recruit supporters and to raise campaign funds; and to obtain maximum news coverage for myself and my stand on the many local and national issues. The most important purpose of all was for me to learn the nation—what it is, and what it ought to be.

When campaigning for the Presidential nomination, Carter appeared before a group of seventeen-year-olds. He addressed his audience as follows:

I grow peanuts over in Georgia. I'm the first child in my daddy's family who ever had a chance. I used to get up at four in the morning to pick peanuts. Then I'd walk three miles along the railroad track to deliver them. My house had no running water or electricity. . . . But I made it to the U.S. Naval Academy and became a nuclear physicist under Admiral Rickover. . . . Then I came back home to the farm and got interested in community affairs. . . . In 1970 I became Governor of Georgia with a campaign that appealed to all people. I reorganized the state government and proved that government could provide love and compassion to all people, black and white—because I believe in it. . . . Now I want to be your President. I hope you'll come see me. Please don't leave me up there in the White House all by myself.

Jackson, Mississippi
December, 1975

Jumping from the platform of the Plains train station.

In a speech Carter talked about Washington and secrecy:
Recently we have discovered that our trust has been betrayed. The vails of secrecy have seemed to thicken around Washington. The purpose and goals of our country are uncertain and sometimes even suspect.

Our people are understandably concerned about this lack of competence and integrity. The root of the problem is not so much that our people have lost confidence in government, but that government has demonstrated time and again its lack of confidence in the people.

Washington, D.C.
December, 1974

In a television interview Carter said:
When I stand out on a factory shift line like I did this morning . . . everybody that comes through there, when I shake hands with them for that instant, I really care about them in a genuine way. And I believe they know it a lot of times. Quite often I will shake hands with a woman who works in a plant, say an older woman, and I just touch her hand, and quite frequently they'll put their arms around my neck and say, "God bless you, son," or "Good luck."

May, 1976

92

Carter wrote about the Presidency as follows:

I have always looked on the Presidency of the United States with reverence and awe, and I still do. But recently I have begun to realize that the President is just a human being. I can almost remember when I began to change my mind and form this opinion.

Before becoming governor I had never met a President, although I once saw Harry Truman at a distance. . . . Then during 1971 and 1972 I met Richard Nixon, Spiro Agnew, George McGovern, Henry Jackson, Hubert Humphrey, Ed Muskie, George Wallace, Ronald Reagan, Nelson Rockefeller, and other Presidential hopefuls, and I lost my feeling of awe about Presidents. This is not meant as a criticism of them, but it is merely a simple statement of fact.

October, 1975

During a television interview Carter said of the way he planned to act as President:

There will be times when I'm asked a question that I might refuse to answer. But if I give an answer, it will be the truth.

May, 1976

In a television interview, Carter was asked what he thought of being called a "wishy-washy" candidate. He answered:

I don't think that the voters are in doubt about what I say; they just feel that I'm the kind of person they can trust, and if they are liberal, I think I'm compatible with their views. If they are moderate, the same; and if the voter is conservative, I think they still feel that I'd be a good President. So I think this is a kind of image that's a good one; it's based on compatibility with voters, not because they've put me in little boxes as a certain sort of ideologically committed person.

Washington, D.C.
March, 1976

After winning the Pennsylvania primary, Carter was asked what he attributed his success to. He answered:

Well, we had a lot of opposition . . . as you know, from the Democratic machine politicians here, but again, I think that put us in a posture of appealing directly to the voters and they kind of rallied behind me in Pennsylvania, as they have in five or six other primaries now. So I think it was the candidate-voter intimate, personal relationship that's proven to be our style and I think the reason we won here.

Philadelphia, Pennsylvania
April, 1976

In a television interview Carter said:

There's only one person in this nation that can speak with a clear voice for the American people. There's only one person who can set a standard of ethics and morality and excellence and greatness—or calling on the American people to make a sacrifice—and explain the purpose of the sacrifice—or answer difficult questions and propose and carry out bold programs—or provide for a defense posture that will make us feel secure, a foreign policy that makes us proud once again—and that's the President.

May, 1976

During the New Hampshire primary, Carter said in a television interview:

The people want someone they can trust. The biggest issue in this campaign is what is the relationship going to be, beginning next January, between the people ourselves, who have been deeply wounded and hurt and disappointed and disillusioned by what's going on in Washington, and our government in Washington that we really love. And they want someone they can trust, someone who's competent, who can manage the affairs of government. I think they look on me as being that kind of candidate, at least so far.

February, 1976

Speaking before a rally, Carter talked about being an outsider:

I can tell you that there is a major and fundamental issue taking shape in this election year. That issue is the division between the "insiders" and the "outsiders." I have been accused of being an outsider. I plead guilty. Unfortunately, the vast majority of Americans—like almost everyone in this room—are also outsiders.

Boston, Massachusetts
July, 1976

Jimmy Carter, during a television interview, was asked, "What drives you?" He answered:

I don't know . . . exactly how to express it. As I said, it's not an unpleasant sense of being driven. I feel like I have one life to live. I feel like that God wants me to do the best I can with it. And that's quite often my major prayer. Let me live my life so that it will be meaningful. And I enjoy attacking difficult problems and solving of solutions and answering the difficult questions and the meticulous organization of a complicated effort. It's a challenge—possibly it's like a game. I don't know. I don't want to lower it by saying it's just a game, but it's an enjoyable thing for me.

May, 1976

Speaking before the National Press Club, Carter discussed political leaders who were isolated from the people:

They have made decisions from an ivory tower. Few have ever seen personally the direct impact of government programs involving welfare, prisons, mental institutions, unemployment, school busing, or public housing. Our people feel that they have little access to the core of government and little influence with elected officials.

Washington, D.C.

Carter expressed his views on Christianity and the Presidency during a television interview:

I don't look on the Presidency as a pastorate. . . . No. Althought Teddy Roosevelt said it's a bully pulpit, no, I don't look on it with religious connotations. But it gives me a chance to serve, and it also gives me a chance to magnify whatever influence I have, for either good or bad, and I hope it will be for the good.

May, 1976

Before a Cincinnati labor convention, Carter gave one of his finest speeches during his campaign for the Democratic Presidential nomination:

I am running for President because I have a vision of a new America, a different America, a better America, and it is not shared by those who are trying so hard to stop my campaign.

97

I have a vision of an America that is, in Bob Dylan's phrase, busy being born, not dying.

I see an America that is poised not only at the brink of a new century, but at the dawn of a new era of responsive, responsible government.

I see an America that has turned her back on scandals and corruption and official cynicism and finally demanded a government that deserves the trust and respect of her people.

I see an America with a tax system that is responsive to its people, and with a system of justice that is evenhanded to all.

I see a government that does not spy on its citizens, but respects your dignity and your privacy and your right to be let alone.

I see an America in which law and order is not a slogan, but a way of life, because our people have chosen to bind up our wounds and live in harmony.

I see an America in which your child and my child and every child, regardless of background, receives an education that will permit full development of talents and abilities.

I see an America that has a job for every man and woman who wants to work.

I see an America that will reconcile its need for new energy sources with its need for clean air, clean water, and an environment we can pass on with pride to our children and their children.

I see an American foreign policy that is as consistent and generous as the American people and that can once again be a beacon for the hopes of the whole world.

I see an America on the move again, united, its

wounds healed, its head high—an America with pride in its past and faith in its future, moving into its third century with confidence and competence and compassion, an America that lives up to the nobility of its constitution and the decency of its people.

I see America with a President who does not govern by vetoes and negativism, but with vigor and vision and positive, affirmative, aggressive leadership.

This is my vision of America.

It is one that reflects the deepest feelings of millions of people who have supported me this year. It is from you that I take my strength and my hope and my courage as I carry forth my campaign toward its ultimate success.

Thank you, God bless you.

Cincinnati, Ohio

In a speech delivered before the National Press Club, Carter said:

I am convinced that among us 200 million Americans there is a willingness—even eagerness—to restore in our country what has been lost—*if* we have understandable purposes and goals and a modicum of bold and inspired leadership.

Our government can express the highest common ideals of human beings—*if* we demand of it standards of excellence.

It is now time to stop and to ask ourselves the question which my last commanding officer, Admiral Hyman

Rickover, asked me and every other naval officer who serves or has served in an atomic submarine. For our nation—for all of us—that question is, Why not the best?

Washington, D.C.
December, 1974

During an interview, Carter was accused of trying to be all things to all people. His response was:
As I have said many times, if there is ever evidence that I have changed my position from one place to another, it would be suicidal because ever since early in January I have had the constant attention of the national news media—and if there was ever any evidence put forward that I took a different position in one part of the country to another from one month to another, it would be political suicide and I don't intend to commit that suicide and don't have any inclination to equivocate or to mislead anybody.

May, 1976

Speaking at a dinner, Jimmy Carter said:
In history we have been taught that it has almost always been impossible to combine freedom and individuality and liberty on one hand and equality on the other. . . . Our country has made that promise. It is a fumbling, struggling, often a mistaken promise, but I think we are getting closer.

Atlanta, Georgia

While running for the Democratic Presidential nomination, Jimmy Carter said:

Watch me closely during the campaign, because I won't be any better a President than I am a candidate.

After observing a number of politicians, who admittedly enjoyed a few drinks at the end of the day, Carter said:

Being elected President was more important to me than a drink before dinner.

During the hectic days of campaigning for the Democratic Presidential nomination, Carter's aide Charles Kirbo teased him about the easy life of the traveling man. Carter responded:

See if you can help me. They're going to break me down or they're going to kill me.

At a press conference, Carter talked about running for President:

I think that anybody who aspires to higher office such as the Presidency would have to have a high opinion of themselves. I think probably politicians are about half ego and about half humility. I think I have my share of both of them.

Little Rock, Arkansas
April, 1975

During a conversation with reporters, Carter acknowledged that Lyndon Johnson had never been fully accepted by the eastern liberals. "Why," he was asked, "would you think you could be?" Carter replied:

Because I am sure of myself.

June, 1976

After a triumphant victory in Pennsylvania's pivotal primary, Carter said:

Most of my attitude toward government is very aggressive. I wouldn't be a quiescent or a timid President.

Discussing Watergate during an interview, Carter said:

I think the American people understand Watergate; I think they're sick of it. I think they've been embarrassed by it. They can make their own judgments about whether or not Ford and Nixon had a previous agreement concerning the pardon. I take Ford at his word that there was no secret agreement.

For me to raise the question would be a divisive thing. I think it's an emotional issue and I don't think it would be a reason for me to accrue political advantage and I don't think it would be healthy for the country. So I don't intend to raise the Watergate issue.

Madison, Wisconsin
March, 1976

*Carter said he welcomed the ordeal of the primaries be-
cause he knew he had to prove himself:*

I want to be tested in the most severe way. . . . I
want the American people to understand my character,
my weakness, the kind of person I am.

*Carter, while running for the Democratic Presidential
nomination, said:*

The people of this country want a fresh face, not
one associated with a long series of mistakes made at the
White House and on Capitol Hill. The next President
of the United States will be the man who can convince a
disillusioned America that he is not of that old school,
but that government can work and be decent.

December, 1975

*The most frequent question Carter got while campaigning
in 1976 for the Presidential nomination was, "Are you
serious?" His answer was:*

I don't intend to lose.

*When Carter was campaigning in New Hampshire, a man
asked him whether he was liberal, conservative, or moderate. Carter replied:*

I don't like to categorize. I don't see myself as a
liberal or conservative or the like.

I'm a farmer, you know. Now, you ask most farmers
whether they are liberal or conservative, and they often

say conservative. The same with businessmen. And I'm a businessman, too. But that isn't to say all businessmen and all farmers are conservative.

New Hampshire
January, 1976

At a rally, Carter said:
There's going to be more scrutiny by the press, more attacks by the other candidates. If I can't stand up, I don't deserve to be President. Be high in your standards. Be tough in your criticism.

Salem, New Hampshire
January, 1976

Campaigning through Illinois Carter said:
It's difficult to label me, I realize. But it's equally difficult to narrowly define any individual.

February, 1976

Before fifteen hundred delegates attending a national League of Women Voters Convention, Carter talked about tax inequities:
For too long the Congress has been committed—perhaps almost by default, perhaps almost without realizing it—to preserving the privileged status of powerful special interest groups in the tax field.

May, 1976

Speaking before the Cleveland City Club, Carter had the following to say about America:

Our nation is still very strong, the strongest on earth —militarily, economically, politically—primarily because of our people. But in recent years we have been hurt, disillusioned, by some of the things that have gone on in our government. That is not an anti-Washington statement. I hope to move to Washington next January, but to correct mistakes is important. We have seen some precious things slip out of our grasp. We have seen the damaging effect of an unnecessary war in Vietnam and Cambodia, contrived and evolved in secret. We've seen a President disgraced and our nation disgraced in the process. We've seen friendly governments overthrown by unwarranted interference by our own forces or secret agents. We've learned about murder and assassinations being plotted in a time of peace by an official agency of our government. These things ought to be rooted out, and I believe that 1976 is a time when it might best be done, not because I am a candidate but because, first of all, it is the celebration of our 200th anniversary. We have a strong inclination now and are constantly reminded to search back in our affairs to see what is best and to preserve it, to see what is wrong and to eliminate it. We ought to study individually the composition of our government, its unrealized potential, as we have been doing through the years; and the repository of that ability lies in one place only.

Cleveland, Ohio
April, 1976

In a speech given at a AFL-CIO convention, Carter said:
My critics don't want to stop Carter. They want to stop the reforms I am committed to. They want to stop the people of this country from regaining control of their government. They want to preserve the status quo, to preserve politics as usual, to maintain at all costs their own entrenched, unresponsive, bankrupt, irresponsible political power.

They know I do not believe in business as usual or politics as usual or a blind acceptance of the status quo.

May, 1976

While seeking the Democratic Presidential nomination, Carter appeared before a group in Cincinnati and was asked a joking question about peanuts. He replied:
I think a lot of people have become more aware of the presence of peanuts in this country this year. I think that the image of a peanut, which is a crop that I grow, being kind of small and insignificant, but cumulatively being very important to the American people, is one that fairly accurately mirrors the kind of campaign that we've run.

Running for President

Refuting President Ford's accusations, Carter sent him a telegram that said:

You have made erroneous statements about my position on several important issues:

One. I do not advocate increasing income taxes on low or middle income families. Two. I do not advocate eliminating the existing home owner income tax credits. Three. I do not advocate new spending programs which would cost anything near $100 billion. My pledge is to have a balanced budget by 1980 and to phase in new programs only as funds become available through an expanding economy and improved government management. Four. I do not advocate a $15 billion reduction in the defense budget. My projected savings from efficiency and elmination of waste is from $5 billion to $7 billion.

I am sure that after these corrections, you, as a man of integrity, will refrain from making these misleading and erroneous statements to the American people.

October, 1976

Speaking about great Democratic Presidents of the past, Carter said in his acceptance speech before the Democratic National Convention:

Ours is the party of a man who was nominated by those different conventions, and who inspired and restored the nation in its darkest hours: Franklin D. Roosevelt.

Ours is a party of a fighting Democrat who showed us that a common man could be an uncommon leader: Harry S Truman.

Ours is a party of a brave young President who called the young at heart regardless of age, to seek a new frontier of national greatness: John F. Kennedy.

And ours is also the party of a great-hearted Texan, who took office in a tragic hour and who went on to do more than any other President in this century to advance the cause of human rights: Lyndon Johnson.

New York City
July, 1976

In his acceptance speech for the Democratic nomination for the Presidency, Jimmy Carter said:

Nineteen seventy-six will not be a year of politics as usual. It can be a year of inspiration and hope and it will be a year of concern, a quiet and sober reassessment of our nation's character and purpose, a year when voters already have confounded the experts, and I guarantee you

Talking with his brother Billy at a barbecue in Plains.

that it will be the year we give the government of this country back to the people of this country.

New York City
July, 1976

At the Democratic convention, Carter said:
Well, I've read parts of the embarrassing transcripts, and I've seen the proud statement of a former Attorney General, who protected his boss, and now brags on the fact that he tiptoed through a mine field and came out "clean." I can't imagine somebody like Thomas Jefferson tiptoeing through a mine field on the technicalities of the law, and then bragging about being clean afterwards.

I think our people demand more than that. I believe that everyone in this room who is in a position of responsibility as a preserver of the law in its purest form ought to remember the oath that Thomas Jefferson and others took when they practically signed their own death warrant, writing the Declaration of Independence—to preserve justice and equity and freedom and fairness, they pledged their lives, their fortunes, and their sacred honor.

New York City
July, 1976

Speaking before the Public Citizen Forum, Carter said:
A lot of news media representatives and sociologists and political science professors have asked, "Are you a liberal or a conservative?" I never have tried to answer

the question. In some areas I would be quite liberal: in consumer protection, environmental quality, human rights, and civil rights. In other areas I would be quite conservative: tight management of government, careful planning, strengthening of local government, good openness of government. One way to categorize my beliefs would be popularism, if you would let me define the word —and I would almost equate it with consumerism. I have been deeply hurt, as have many other Americans in the last few years, by the deterioration and the quality of our governmental processes. They have been demonstrated in many minor ways, but in a few major ways: the Vietnamese and Cambodian wars; the attempt to become involved in Angola; the CIA revelations; the Watergate scandals. There has been a deep sense of alienation of people from our government and a sense of disappointment, a sense of embarassment—sometimes even a sense of shame. These feelings, perhaps, are justified and legitimate, but there is a reservoir of deep commitment that exists in the minds and hearts of the American people that is waiting to be tapped. I have always felt that, to the extent that government in all its forms can equal the character of the American people—to that extent, our wrongs can be redressed, our mistakes corrected, the difficult answers can, perhaps, be given to difficult questions, and there can be a restoration of confidence of people in government.

Washington, D.C.
August, 1976

113

In the first of three television debates, Carter said:

Well, tonight we've had a chance to talk a lot about the past. But I think it's time to talk about the future.

Our nation in the last eight years has been divided as never before. It's a time for unity. It's a time to draw ourselves together. To have a President and a Congress that can work together with mutual respect, for a change, cooperating for a change in the open for a change. So the people can understand their own government.

For a long time our American citizens have been excluded, sometimes misled, sometimes have been lied to. This is not compatible with the purpose of our nation.

I believe in our country. It needs to be competent. The government needs to be well-managed, efficient, economical. We need to have a government that's sensitive to our people's needs—to those who are poor, who don't have adequate health care, who have been cheated too long with our tax programs, who've been out of jobs, whose families have been torn apart.

We need to restore the faith and the trust of the American people in their own government.

In addition to that, we've suffered because we haven't had leadership in the administration. We've got a government of stalemate. We've lost the vision of what our country can and ought to be.

This is not the America that we've known in the past. It's not the America that we have to have in the future.

I don't claim to know all the answers. But I've got confidence in my country. Our economic strength is still there. Our system of government—in spite of Vietnam, Cambodia, CIA, Watergate—is still the best system of government on earth.

And the greatest resource of all are the two hundred and fifteen million Americans who still have within us the strength, the character, the intelligence, the experience, the patriotism, the idealism, the compassion, the sense of brotherhood on which we can rely in the future to restore the greatness to our country.

We ought not to be excluded from our government any more. We need a President that can go in who derives his strength from the people. I owe the special interests nothing. I owe everything to you, the people of this country.

And I believe that we can bind our wounds. I believe that we can tap the tremendous untapped reservoir of innate strength in this country. That we can once again have a government as good as our people and let the world know what we still know and hope for—that we still live in the greatest and the strongest and the best country on earth.

Philadelphia, Pennsylvania
September, 1976

In his acceptance speech at the Democratic convention, Carter said:
It will be the year we give the government of this country back to the people of this country. . . . I have spoken a lot of times this year about love. But love must be aggressively translated into simple justice.

New York City
July, 1976

115

Discussing civil law and God's law in a magazine inter-view, Carter said:

I believe people should honor civil laws. If there is a conflict between God's law and civil law, we should honor God's law. But we should be willing to accept civil punishment. Most of Christ's original followers were killed because of their belief in Christ; they violated the civil law in following God's law. Reinhold Niebuhr, a theologian who has dealt with this problem at length, says that the framework of law is a balancing of forces in a society: the law itself tends to alleviate tension brought about by these forces. But the laws on the books are not a measure of this balance nearly as much as the degree to which the laws are enforced. So when a law is anachronistic and is carried over from a previous age, it's just not observed.

Plains, Georgia
November, 1976

During the Democratic convention, Carter said at the close of his acceptance speech:

We *can* have an America that has turned away from scandal and corruption and official cynicism and is once again as decent and competent as our people . . . an American government that does not oppress or spy on its people . . . an American President who does not govern with negativism and fear for the future . . . a President

116

who's not isolated from the people but who feels your pain and shares your dreams and takes his strength and courage from you.

> *New York City*
> *July, 1976*

When interviewed by a magazine, Carter talked about running for the Presidency:
I don't feel uneasy about the job. I don't know why —I just don't.

> *September, 1976*

Talking to a group of economic advisors, Carter said:
Think about four years, think about eight years. Give me programs that are bold. I think I'm going to win with a great mandate.

> *Plains, Georgia*
> *Summer, 1976*

Asked during a magazine interview whether the public could expect a puritanical tone to be set in the White House if Carter were elected President, he replied:
Harry Truman was a Baptist. Some people get very abusive about the Baptist faith. If people want to know about it, they can read the New Testament. The main thing is that we don't think we're better than anyone

else. . . . I can't change the teachings of Christ. I can't change the teachings of Christ! I believe in them and a lot of people in this country do as well. Jews believe in the Bible. They have the same Commandments.

Plains, Georgia
November, 1976

While campaigning, Carter talked about his vulnerability in the forthcoming election:
My major vulnerability is that people still don't know who I am or what I stand for on specific issues. Although I was in all [but one] of the primaries, I mostly restricted my efforts to just a few states. I still have never campaigned extensively in California, Massachusetts, or New York. We organized only three states in depth—Iowa, Florida, and New Hampshire—and did a lesser, but effective, job in Ohio and Pennyslvania.

The major issue used by my primary opponents, particularly Congressman Morris Udall, was that I was fuzzy on the issues. The constant campaign statement had an impact in some of the states, although not the majority. But we have a fairly good public opinion poll and this has paid rich dividends—not in shaping stands on issues, because those cannot be modified—but in the orientation of our responses: where I spend my time, where we spend our money, where I could send my wife or one of my children.

New York City
July 19, 1976

In answer to the question "What kind of President do you want to be?" Carter gave the following reply:

I'd like to be a President who is both competent and inspirational, who could be incisive in his analysis of the major problems of the nation, who could arouse support for the solution of those problems among a broad base of American citizens. I'd like to arrive at a maximum degee of harmony.

July, 1976

Carter said to a conference of Democratic state chairmen:

I am no big shot. I am not anybody's boss. I want to be everybody's servant.

Washington, D.C.
August, 1976

Returning to Plains triumphant after winning the Democratic Presidential nomination, Carter said to the people who greeted him:

I've met a lot of folks around the country—people just like us, people who know what it means to have to work for a living, who live close to one another, who have deep religious faith, who love their schools, who want to see their kids have a better chance in life than we have, who love this country, who have been disappointed at some of the things that have happened here, who want to see it better, who want to see us correct our mistakes, who want to see the divisions that have existed, some-

119

times, among us eliminated once and for all, and who look back two hundred years ago and try to understand what the founders of our nation dreamed about—and make those dreams come true.

Plains, Georgia
July, 1976

Jimmy Carter explained in an interview what populism means to him:

My strength comes directly from the populace. Any decision I make must, of course, be objective and fair— to redress grievances and overcome the last vestiges of the consequences of racial discrimination. In the future . . . support must come from the population as a whole.

August, 1976

In a magazine interview, Carter said:

On human rights, civil rights, environmental quality, I consider myself to be very liberal. On the management of government, on openness of government, on strengthening individual liberties and local levels of government, I consider myself a conservative. And I don't see that the two attitudes are incompatible.

Plains, Georgia
November, 1976

Carter talked during an interview about the role that Congress must play in safeguarding the President from his own tendencies toward imperial power:

I relish open conflict a little too much. I don't know why I like it so much, but I do. But I shall try instead a strategy of involving the legislators in the initial stages of the legislation so as not to confront them with a decision they'd have to accept, reject, or be bargained into. And Congress shall also be a partner in the making of foreign policy. And I shall propose that all my Cabinet members present themselves to the Congress in a joint session to answer questions, the way they do in the British system. And if they withhold information not relating to national security, I will get rid of them.

Plains, Georgia
November, 1976

Carter, speaking at the Alfred E. Smith Memorial Dinner, said:

We are, of course, a nation of immigrants, but some of us too often forget that fact. Sometimes we forget that the question isn't when we came here, but why we came here.

Our nation has been called a melting pot. I think of it more as a mosaic, one to which many groups make their own distinct contribution.

New York City
October, 1976

121

In a magazine interview, Carter made the statement:

I will never make a private commitment to any legislator that cannot be made public.

Plains, Georgia
November, 1976

Carter was asked during an interview whether those who had first supported him would receive special consideration in his appointments. He took his answer from St. Matthew:

My feelings are those of the man who went out early in the morning to hire workers to harvest wheat and told them he would pay them five dollars to work in his field that day. Then he went out at nine and at twelve and again at five and hired three more groups, each with the same promise. And at the end of the day he called them all in and he paid the last first and he paid them all the same. Those who'd come first said it wasn't fair, since they'd worked longer, but the man said he had done no wrong so long as he had kept the promise he made to each of them, which he had. And the point Christ was making was that latecomers would be acceptable to God on an equal basis with those who early in life worked in His kingdom.

I appreciate the people who've been with me from the start before it was fashionable, but I hope their sense of contribution is reward enough. And those who've come late ought not be discriminated against. What matters is each person, and each covenant on its own merits.

Plains, Georgia
November, 1976

America and the World

Carter was asked during an interview if it was possible to reduce inflation and unemployment simultaneously. He answered:

Yes, I think so. The rough cost of welfare and unemployment compensation is about $20 billion. I think we should encourage increased employment, primarily through the private sector, but with some government instigation—using part of that $20 billion in expanding housing starts and transportation and energy research and development. This will result in lower unemployment and in both a relatively constant inflation rate—no higher than four percent yearly—and an annual increase in the gross national product of four to six percent.

Plains, Georgia
October, 1976

In an interview Carter was asked how he would restore trust in government. He answered:

I would do everything I could to open up the government to the people. I would hold frequent cross-examination press conferences. I would minimize the "palace guard" orientation of the White House staff. . . . I would also make all appointments on the basis of merit and not as a political payoff.

Plains, Georgia
October, 1976

During a television debate with President Ford at the Walnut Street Theater, Carter talked about the tax structure:

The present tax structure is a disgrace. . . . It's just a welfare program for the rich. As a matter of fact, twenty-five percent of the total tax reductions go for only one percent of the richest people. And over fifty percent of the tax credits go for fourteen percent of the richest people. . . . The whole philosophy of the Republican party has been to pile on taxes on the low-income people and to take them off on the corporations.

Philadelphia, Pennsylvania
September, 1976

In a television debate between Ford and Carter, Carter talked about China:

In the Far East I think we need to continue to be strong, and I would certainly pursue the normalization of relationships with the People's Republic of China.

126

Sightseeing in Washington before the election, with
daughter Amy and wife Rosalynn.

We opened up a great opportunity in 1972, which has pretty well been frittered away under Mr. Ford, but I would never let the friendship with the People's Republic of China stand in the way of the preservation of the independence and freedom of the people of Taiwan.

San Francisco, California
October, 1976

In a ninety-minute debate with Ford on national television, Carter talked about our foreign policy. He said of Kissinger:

Mr. Kissinger has been the President of this country. Mr. Ford has shown an absence of leadership, and an absence of a grasp of what this country is and what it ought to be. That's got to be changed. And that's one of the major issues in this campaign of 1976.

San Francisco, California
October, 1976

Discussing embargos in a debate with President Ford, Carter said:

I would never single out food as a trade embargo item, if I ever decided to impose an embargo because of a crisis in international relationships. It would include all shipments of all equipment.

For instance, if the Arab countries ever again declare an embargo against our nation on oil, I would consider that not a military but an economic declaration of war and I would respond instantly and in kind. I would not ship that Arab country anything—no weapons, no spare parts for weapons, no oil-drilling rigs, no oil pipe, no nothing. I wouldn't just single out food.

San Francisco, California
October, 1976

Carter expressed his views on television about the missing in Vietnam during a debate with President Ford:

One of the most embarrassing failures of the Ford administration and one that touches specifically on human rights, is his refusal to appoint a Presidential commission to go to Vietnam, to go to Laos, to go to Cambodia, and try to trade for the release of information about those who are missing in action in those wars. This is what the families of MIAs want. So far Mr. Ford has not done it.

San Francisco, California
October, 1976

Discussing the "sunshine law," Carter said the following in his "For America's Third Century, Why Not Our Best?" speech:

We need an all-inclusive sunshine law in Washington so that special interests will not retain their exclusive access behind closed doors. Except in a few rare cases, there is no reason for secret meetings of regulatory agencies, other executive departments or congressional committees. Such meetings must be opened to the public, all votes recorded, and complete news media coverage authorized and encouraged.

Washington, D.C.
December, 1974

On the subject of taxes, Carter said in his speech announcing his candidacy for the Democratic Presidential nomination:

Gross tax inequities are being perpetuated. The most surely taxed income is that which is derived from the sweat of manual labor. Carefully contrived loopholes let the total tax burden shift more and more toward the average wage earner. The largest corporations pay the lowest tax rates and some with very high profits pay no tax at all.

When a business executive can charge off a fifty-dollar luncheon on a tax return and a truck driver cannot deduct his $1.50 sandwich—when oil companies pay less than five percent on their earnings while employees of the company pay at least three times this rate—when many pay no tax on incomes of more than $100,000—then we need basic tax reform!

Washington, D.C.
December, 1974

Discussing integration and schools, Carter said during a television interview:

I think that the passage of the Civil Rights Act was the best thing that ever happened to the South in my lifetime. The integration of our schools has not been a step backward for us; it has been a step forward. I think we've made a lot of progress in the South, and I think most Southerners are proud of it. I'm not in favor of mandatory busing. We tried it in the South, and it didn't work. The only kids that ever got bused were the poor children. I've never seen a rich child bused. So we worked out in Atlanta a busing system that is my favorite, and I would emphasize this, but I've also made it clear that as President, I would be sworn to uphold the law, and if the federal courts ruled contrary to my own personal desire, that I would support the federal courts. Also, I do not favor a constitutional amendment to prohibit busing. I think it would be a very divisive thing.

New York City
March, 1976

In a TV interview Carter said the following about government agencies:

Well, there is no way for me to envision at this point as a full-time candidate which particular agencies in the federal government would survive three years after I'm in the White House. It took me a full year just to study Georgia's government, when we had 300 agencies to start with; we abolished 278 of them, through consolidation or complete elimination. But we now have about 1,900,

131

perhaps more, in the federal government, and I intend to cut those down to no more than 200. It's a goal that I've set for myself that I think is achievable.

New York City
March, 1976

Carter discussed his views on abortion in an interview:
I have a deep feeling that abortion is wrong. At what stage in the development of the fetus it becomes murder, I can't say. But I wish that there were never any abortions. It really bothers me about it. The Supreme Court has ruled that the first thirteen weeks the mother [has] a right to have an abortion. I wish that there were no abortions but I can't say at what point the abortion becomes murder.

March, 1976

In a TV interview, Carter talked about foreign policy:
When I've been in foreign countries, and gone into the embassies, it's obvious from talking to the people in the countries, and talking to the ambassadors, that they are not qualified to be diplomats for this country. They are all appointed as a political payoff. The point I make is that whether they are actually fat or thin, that they are appointed because there are political interrelationships and not because of quality. Now, the last time I was in

132

Europe, for instance, out of 33 ambassadors who served in the whole European theater, only three of them were professional diplomats. The others were appointed for political reasons.

New York City
March, 1976

Speaking on the subject of regulatory agencies in Washington, Carter said:
The regulatory agencies in Washington are made up, not of people to regulate industries, but of representatives of the industries that are regulated. Is that fair and right and equitable? I don't think so.

Athens, Georgia
May, 1974

In a major speech before an audience in New Hampshire, Carter discussed the family structure:
We are going to reverse the trend that we've experienced in the past that has destroyed the American family. . . . I believe we can restore what was lost. I believe we can bind our people back together. I believe we can restore human values, respect for one another, intimacy, love, respect for the law, patriotism, good education, strong churches, a good relationship among

133

our people and government. I pledge to you that every statement I make, every decision I make, will give our families a decent chance to be strong again.

Manchester, New Hampshire
August, 1976

Talking to a television audience of 85 million about the criminal justice system, Carter said:
The big shots who are rich or influential very seldom go to jail; those who are poor and who have no influence quite often are the ones who are punished. And the whole subject of crime is one that concerns our people very much and I believe that the fairness of it is a major problem that addresses our leader and this is something that hasn't been addressed adequately by this administration.

But I hope to have a complete responsibility on my shoulders to help bring about a fair criminal justice system and also to bring about an end to the divisiveness that has occurred in our country as a result of the Vietnam war.

Philadelphia, Pennsylvania
September, 1976

Jimmy Carter expressed his views on amnesty for Vietnam draft evaders before an audience of American Legionaires:
Where I came from most of the men who went off to fight in Vietnam were poor. They didn't know where

134

Canada was, they didn't know where Sweden was, they didn't have the money to hide from the draft in college. Many of them thought it was a bad war, but they went anyway. A lot of them came back with scarred minds or bodies, or with missing limbs. Some didn't come back at all. . . .

I could never equate what they have done with those who left this country to avoid the draft. But I think it is time for the damage, hatred, and divisiveness of the Vietnam war to be over.

I do not favor a blanket amnesty, but for those who violated selective service laws, I intend to grant a blanket pardon.

To me, there is a difference. Amnesty means that what you did is right. A pardon means that what you did —right or wrong—is forgiven. So—pardon, yes; amnesty, no.

For deserters, each case should be handled on an individual basis in accordance with our nation's system of military justice.

Seattle, Washington
August, 1976

Carter expressed his views on busing in a newspaper interview:

I favor school integration. I do not favor mandatory busing.

The only kids who get bused are the poor children. I've never seen a rich child bused. The rich parents either move or put the kid in private schools.

135

We worked out a system in Atlanta, which I personally favor. Any child that wants to be bused can be bused, but the busing must contribute to increased integration. The black leadership must be adequately represented in the decision-making process of the school system at all levels. And no child is bused against the wishes of the child.

But if the federal courts should rule differently from my preference while I'm in the White House, I would support the federal courts; and I do not favor any constitutional amendment to prohibit busing.

April, 1976

Discussing our relationship with the Soviet Union as viewed by our western European allies, Carter said in a speech before the Foreign Policy Assocation:

We need to recognize also that in recent years our western European allies have been deeply concerned, and justly so, by our unilateral dealings with the Soviet Union. To the maximum extent possible, our dealings with the Communist powers should reflect the combined views of the democracies, and thereby avoid suspicions by our allies that we may be disregarding their interests.

We seek not a condominium of the powerful but a community of the free.

New York City
June, 1976

When speaking about his ethnic views, Carter said during an interview:

People have a tendency—and it is an unshakable tendency—to want to share common special clubs, common churches, common restaurants. I would not use the forces of the federal government to break up the ethnic character of such neighborhoods.

April, 1976

Addressing the Foreign Policy Association, Carter said:

In the area of foreign policy, our people are troubled, confused, and sometimes angry. There has been too much emphasis on transient spectaculars and too little on substance. We are deeply concerned, not only by such obvious tragedies as the war in Vietnam, but by the more subtle erosion in the focus and morality of our foreign policy.

Under the Nixon-Ford administration, there has evolved a kind of secretive "Lone Ranger" foreign policy —a one-man policy of international adventure. This is not an appropriate policy for America.

New York City
June, 1976

In a speech on the Middle East, Carter said:

We all want to see a Middle East dedicated to human progress rather than sterile hate. We want to see the desert bloom on both sides of the river Jordan, and along the

Nile, and everywhere that human beings hope for better lives for themselves and their children.

We must work toward these goals through international organizations as well as negotiations. This is a difficult time for Israel in the international arena, primarily because of the importance of oil to the world's developing nations. I deplore the actions taken recently in the United Nations. I reject utterly the charge that Zionism is a form of racism. Indeed, Zionism was a response to racism against the Jewish people. The concept of a state of Israel was born out of centuries of persecution of human beings because they practiced a different religion.

New York City
April, 1976

When asked where he got his advice on the cities, Carter replied:

Well, I listen to a lot of people. I have 300 or 400 persons now, from the academic world and from within the structure of the mayors' councils, who volunteered to help me. And I deal directly with leaders who happen to serve in public life. Obviously, some of my good advisors would be Henry Maier from Milwaukee, Pete Flaherty from Pittsburgh, and Mayor Beame from New York. My inclination is to combine the practical approach from public officials who have the responsibility to administer municipal affairs with the academic and nationally experienced persons who served in the past in agencies in government.

September, 1976

Addressing the United Nations, Carter had the following to say about the energy problem:

The world has only enough oil to last about 30 to 40 years at the present rate of consumption. It has large coal reserves—with perhaps 200 years of reserves in the United States alone. The United States must shift from oil to coal, taking care about the environmental problems involved in coal production and use. Our country must also maintain strict energy conservation measures, and derive increasing amounts of energy from renewable sources such as the sun.

New York City
May, 1976

Carter talked about Israel during a speech on the Middle East:

A lasting peace must be based on the absolute assurance of Israel's survival and security. I would never yield on that point, and it is very important for us to make this clear to the rest of the world. The survival of Israel is a significant moral principle for the people of the United States. We share democracy in a time when few nations are free. We both enjoy a free press and freedom of expression. We are both nations of immigrants. We share cultural and artistic values. We are friends who admire and respect each other. This country was the first nation to recognize Israel's existence as a country and we must remain the first country to which Israel can turn with assurance.

For all these reasons, as long as I am President, the

139

American people will never sacrifice the security or survival of Israel for barrels of oil. Even if every other nation were forced by the thirst for oil to desert Israel, we in this country—with our resources, our power, and our sense of decency—can and will stand fast.

New York City
April, 1976

Discussing détente before the Chicago Council on Foreign Relations, Carter said:
The core of détente is the reduction in arms. We should negotiate to reduce the present SALT ceilings on offensive weapons before both sides start a new arms race to reach the current maximums, and before new missile systems are tested or committed for production.

Chicago, Illinois
March, 1976

Carter, during an interview aboard a plane flying from Seattle to Des Moines, discussed cities that are becoming less integrated:
Well, one of the important aspects of housing as it relates to community evolution is the legal, constitutional right of a family to live where it pleases, not to be excluded by the residents of a particular community because of race or ethnic background. That would be enforced under my administration. I was aggressive in doing this in Georgia, and it was accepted by the people.

En route to Des Moines, Iowa
September, 1976

140

Carter, addressing the Chicago Council on Foreign Relations, talked about aid to developing nations:

Our program of international aid to developing nations should be redirected so that it meets the minimum human needs of the greatest number of people. This means an emphasis on food, jobs, education, and public health—including access to family planning. The emphasis in aid should be on those countries with a proven ability to help themselves, instead of those that continue to allow enormous discrepancies in living standards among their people. The time has come to stop taxing poor people in rich countries for the benefit of rich people in poor countries.

Chicago, Illinois
March, 1976

During an interview Carter was asked if he felt the full cost of welfare should be picked up by the federal governmen. He replied:

Of the basic welfare package, yes. But I would never remove the constitutional right of a state or city to vote bonus payments, or additional payments, above and beyond what is established as adequate for the whole nation by the Congress.

September, 1976

141